Queening

A study Journal

IGBUKOLU TOBECHUKWU YVONNE

Formatted & Digitally Published
Emphaloz Publishing House
www.emphaloz.com

Queening is a must read by every lady, infact, men should read as well and pass it on to every woman they know.

It is so refreshing to read the story of Esther in such an applicable manner. Tobe did an excellent job in identifying qualities in her life that made her Queening all through life.

This book will equip you understand how to reign and take charge in the place of your assignment. I love the fact that this book is well balanced, as Tobe ensured she geared us with ways to imbibe these qualities in our lives and the need to flee from contracting the Vashti-Cancer predicament... This right here hit me.

What are you waiting for, read and enjoy Queening by Tobe, I call it the, "Must have" manual for every woman and men who loves them.

Pastor Imisi Owolabi

Queening is a manual written in a time as this for every woman who desires to be a queen.

It exemplifies the life of Queen Esther thus helping the reader internalize the principles that worked for her even now.

It is highly insightful, instructive and engaging.

The book is no doubt inspired by the Holy Spirit. It is a must have for all daughters, sisters, wives and friends.

Pastor Tomi Adisa

It's a good book, very simple, easy to read and it's relatable, it's something to refer to from time to time and can also be used to create prayers points.

Funmi Victor-Okigbo

DEDICATION

To God,
You give my life meaning... Thank you!

To my unborn kids,
This book is proof that you can do anything you set your mind to do.
I love you.

To Family,
For staying through the good, not so good and bad.
I love you.

TABLE OF CONTENTS

INTRODUCTION

I never for once thought that a day would come when I would write a book. Yes, I enjoy writing posts for blogs, but a book was not even in my wildest dreams. As a young girl, I wanted to be so many things, a singer, a movie director, but certainly not an author.

This journey started one Saturday evening. I was going through a very tough phase in my life at the time, and it seemed to me like I had lost my identity in Christ as a woman. After days of crying my eyes sore, I didn't know what to do with myself anymore. I picked up my Bible and opened it to the Book of Esther. I had read that book several times before then, but I just felt like that was the place for me to read at that particular point in time.

As I read on, God began to open my eyes to certain attributes of Esther that I had not noticed before. The following day, while observing my quiet time, I just felt a strong urge within me to open my Bible to the book of Esther again and looked at each attribute more carefully, relating it to the life of the Christian lady. I knew I had to share all that I had just discovered, hence this book.

Queening is a must-have for every young lady like me aspiring to dominate and conquer the world.

Sometimes, I just read through some of the pages of this book and still learn something new.

Jesus is our only perfect example. Esther must have had her flaws, but as a queen, she SLAYED!

I am sure that the God that has started this great work and inspired this piece will do much more for you than you can ever imagine! Amen.

So please, read, digest, and enjoy every piece of this great revelation about the life of Esther from God. As you get blessed, be a blessing to another lady out there by sharing this book.

FOREWORD

Queen!

That word is used so often when women encourage each other.

"Go Queen!"

"You've got this, queen!"

"You're perfect, queen!"

And while there is an innate royalty in every woman because we are created in the image of the All-Mighty King, Queening bestows on us a great responsibility that not many talk about; It's a call to be wise, kind, and disciplined. It's a mandate to care about others even when it puts us at risk, and the see beyond ourselves and step into the visions of God.

That's what Tobechukwu has done in her book; she's pointed the sceptre of royalty at every woman or girl who reads this, regardless of your age, race or location. But beyond that, she's reminds us that there is beauty not just in the look of the crown, but in the weight of it.

Laju Iren
The Lord's Storyteller
Lagos, Nigeria, 2021

DEFINING A QUEEN

Definition 1: The female ruler of an independent state, especially one who inherits the position by right of birth- **Source: Oxford English Dictionary**

Definition 2: A woman or something personified as a woman that is foremost or pre-eminent in any respect- **Source: Dictionary.com**

Definition 3: A woman who not only carries herself well but, embodies a sense of greatness through accomplishments, serving others, or representing their community in a positive way- **Anonymous**

Having given the above as definitions of a queen, it is imperative that I point out that the term QUEENING refers to the continuous act of being a queen.

NB: (The term **Queening**, for the purpose of this book, will be viewed based on the above contexts only.)

***

When you hear the word "QUEENING", one of the images that come to your mind is that of a queen in her full regalia.

Once upon a time, my favorite slang, caption and bio on social media was "I'm Queening!"

A Queen is a woman who embodies excellence and exudes greatness in every aspect of her life. She takes charge and is in control of her life and whatever situation she is faced with and in this book, we will be understudying one of the most highly favored queens recorded in man's history, **Queen Esther Hadassah Xerxes**.

QUEEN ESTHER HADASSAH XERXES!

Esther chapter 1

Ever heard of the story of Queen Esther Xerxes? Yes? Great! If you haven't, then let me tell you a little about her. She interestingly has a whole book in the Bible dedicated to her.

This story happened in the city of Persia which is also known as Babylon. The King, Xerxes threw a big party that lasted 180 days for everyone in his province and requested the presence of his Queen – Vashti, at one of the occasions, so he could show off her beauty to his visitors. To be honest, the motive of the King may have been questionable considering that he was drunk, having partied non-stop for days and there was really no telling what he had planned to do to the queen in front of his guests who were also most likely as drunk as he was.

Queen Vashti refused to oblige the King's request and this made him furious. To worsen the case, one of the King's advisers teased that if word got out about the Queen's despicable act, other women in the kingdom would begin to disregard their husbands. This made the King more furious that he dethroned Vashti as Queen and after a period of time, ordered that a search for a new Queen be conducted in his favour.

Now, Esther was one of the maidens who was to be presented before the King as a potential replacement for the ex-queen, Vashti. She was an orphan and one of the Jewish exiles in the city. She lived with her uncle, Mordecai who was the leader of the Jews in Babylon.

Esther found favor before everyone she came in contact with, the King inclusive and eventually, she was made the new Queen of Babylon.

Haman, one of the powerful men in the kingdom had asked the king to authorize a decree to wipe out all the Jews in Babylon because he was unhappy with Mordecai (Esther's uncle) for refusing to bow to him.

The King, who was unaware that his Queen, Esther was also a Jew (as she did not reveal it to him following the instructions of her uncle), authorized the decree.

As soon as Mordecai heard about it, he sent a message to Esther, informing her about Haman's plans to wipe out her people and told her to go plead with the King on behalf of the Jews. Esther was afraid. No one was allowed to go see the King without an invitation; in fact, the last time she saw him was a month before!

Not knowing what other step to take, Esther fasted and prayed alongside her people and eventually summoned enough courage to face the King. The King surprisingly, because Esther had won his heart, spared her for seeing him without an invite and even offered her half of his kingdom for her wishes. But Esther wasn't all about the riches of the kingdom, all she asked for was to have the King and Haman join her for dinner that night. The King agreed. After the dinner, she requested again that the King and Haman join her for a banquet the following night after which she would make her request.

Amidst all these, Haman who had built gallows where he intended to hang Mordecai received orders from the king to give a King's honour to Mordecai for revealing a plot to kill the king. This of course, really upset Haman.

Finally, Esther revealed her identity to the King at the banquet and pleaded with him to spare her people and deliver them from the hands of Haman. This got the King very angry. When he learnt about the gallows Haman had built to hang Mordecai, he ordered that Haman and his family be hung in the gallows instead. This was how the courage and bravery of the beautiful Queen Esther saved the lives of all the Jews in Babylon at that time.

Esther, though flawed, is a good description of a woman that stayed Queening, not minding the background she came from. She was a woman with grace, class and poise who had the fear of God.

She was a brave woman. She was raised ready to face the challenges of life and this prepared her mightily for the challenges of the palace. She faced a major adversity named Haman who wouldn't stop at anything but get her out of the way. She had the fear of God in her and God blessed her with wisdom and the right use of words. This gift helped her to buy the heart of the king and she got everything she asked and even things she didn't ask for.

Esther was someone who was willing to go through the necessary grooming process before meeting the King (her Husband) to ensure she was not found wanting in her duties as a wife (Esther 2:10-12). She didn't throw herself to every Tom, Dick, and Harry that came her way because she knew she was specially designed for her king and he alone was worthy of all the God-deposited goodies she carried.

In the next few chapters, we would be learning lots of qualities Esther had that set her apart from the other maidens; qualities ladies in this generation need to make 'that' difference in this fallen world.

CHAPTER 1

QUEENS ARE MODEST AND MODERATE

*"When it was Esther's turn to go to the king (Esther the daughter of Abihail the uncle of Mordecai, who had adopted her as his daughter), she asked for nothing other than what Hegai, the king's eunuch in charge of the harem, had recommended. Esther, just as she was, won the admiration of everyone who saw her." **(Esther 2:15 MSG)***

In a bid to find another queen, all the virgins in the land were to be presented before the king, after undergoing certain purifications and the king was expected to choose the one that he finds as the fairest of them all.

The virgins were expected to go through beauty treatment sessions for months with Hegai, the king's chamberlain to make them "king-worthy".

However, we see from the above text that Esther, who was one of the virgins presented to the king chose to apply moderation in all she did by not asking for anything extra from the king's chamberlain besides what was required, even though she had the opportunity to do so. She was modest.

Being moderate simply means being reasonable in the way we do things; not going extreme. It doesn't always have to do with our dressing/makeup alone. There are a whole lot of other things that humans need to be moderate about. There is a lot of superfluity in the world today. It's almost impossible to talk about modesty or moderation in the world today without getting backlashed or tagged as being judgmental but the truth needs to be said regardless. In order to be the center of attention, many women go almost naked! Call me old school, but I am part of the school of thought that believes some parts of the body should be kept private for personal and spousal viewing only.

The world has tried to make it "cool" for a woman to expose certain parts of her body, they say it's us being confident in our own skin. Little wonder most of the women you see in commercials and the media in general are almost naked.

Let me be clear, it is not a sin to look good. In fact, I believe believers should be at the forefront of everything good including fashion. There is absolutely nothing wrong with Christians being fashion icons as long as it is being done in a godly and decent way. I believe God was the first fashion designer. The Bible tells us He made clothes from skins to cover up the **nakedness** of Adam and Eve (Genesis 3:21). Everything, including the way you dress, must be done in moderation. You shouldn't take glory in your physical appearances than what you have on the inside.

You must learn to do what is required and necessary. For instance, it is necessary for human beings to eat in order to survive. But when a person decides to stuff himself with food, even when he is not hungry, he is not being reasonable.

Esther required nothing more than what the king's chamberlain, Hegai deemed necessary. She did not ask for extra fragrances, more attires, food, makeup, or more maids than what was required. In a bid to be moderate, you should also try not to under-do things. For instance, do not refuse to buy necessary toiletries like deodorants and the likes because you are trying to be moderate. You will only end up having an offensive body odour.

The Bible makes it clear that God loves His children being decent and moderate in all things. Philippians 4:4b says:

> *"Let our moderation be known to all men. The Lord is at hand."*

It is important to also note that when talking about moderation, you must remember the word abstinence. As a believer, there are some things you cannot be moderate in doing, you have to totally abstain from them. For instance, talking about being moderate in the way you smoke weed or fornicate sounds ridiculous because you are expected to abstain from doing such things.

Finally, you must endeavor to check your motives for doing anything. Honestly, that is what sets the basis and also distinguishes the art of moderation from superfluity. If your motives are pure, you will know it within yourself and vice versa. Your actions should be backed up with reasons that are godly.

MY CONFESSIONS:

I, Queen (insert your name) confess that I am a woman of valor.

I understand the importance of being moderate in all things.

I understand that all things are lawful for me but not all things are helpful to me.

I choose to check my motive for doing things at all times.

I choose to only do things that agree with the standard in God's word.

I choose to show moderation in the way I eat, talk, sleep, dress and in all other areas of my life.

I will also pass on this quality to my offspring as it is my responsibility to train them with the right mindset.

My level of exposure is not based on how revealing my outfits are.

My value isn't totally based on my outward appearance. I carry more treasures on my inside.

So, it doesn't matter what the world's standard is, God's desire is that I apply moderation in all things.

Therefore, from today and for the rest of my life, I begin to make conscious efforts at achieving moderation in all aspects of my life as the Holy Spirit guides me.

AMEN

CHAPTER 2

QUEENS ARE RESPECTFUL, SUBMISSIVE TO GOD & THEIR PARTNERS

"Esther continued to keep her family background and nationality a secret. She was still following Mordecai's directions, just as she did when she lived in his home" **(Esther 2:20 NLT).**

I like to think of myself as a Feminist when it's being defined as a quest for the political, economic and social equality of the sexes. Some may argue that Christianity and feminism are not compatible but I strongly believe they are. I however agree that the term feminism has been abused with many using it as a covering to carry out radical and hate causes that do not reflect the true ideology behind being a feminist.

Contrary to popular belief, feminism doesn't seek to bring down the male gender, it just seeks equal social, political and economic rights with the male gender. I believe God was the first feminist. He created woman and gave her equal dignity with man. Genesis 1:27-28 says:

"So *God created man in His own image, in the image of God created He him; male and female created* **them**. *And God blessed* **them**, *and God said unto* **them**, *be fruitful and multiply and replenish the earth and subdue it; and have dominion over the fish of the sea, and over all the fowl of the air, and over every living thing that moveth upon the earth*"

Notice how in the above scripture, God was talking to "**THEM**" i.e. both the male and female. He gave both man and woman the mantle of rulership. He was pro gender-equality and if you know even a little about God, you will know He does not change.

The Bible talks about women being submissive to their spouses and many have argued that it is impossible to be a feminist and still uphold the biblical principle of submission. It is very possible! Firstly, Peter in 1 Peter 3:4-6, taught that women should submit to their husbands, not ALL men! No other man has the right to make a woman submit to him. This also doesn't mean that the woman is less than their husband, they are both joint heirs in Christ. Look at it this way, Jesus submitted to God the father; it however doesn't make Him any less than God!

Peter in his first epistle urged young individuals to submit themselves unto the elders and also to be clothed with humility- (1Peter 5:5).

As a believer, you are also expected to submit to God. James 4:7 says:

> *"...submit yourselves therefore to God. Resist the devil, and he will flee from you"*

From that verse, you see that your ability to resist the devil and his tactics solely relies on your ability to submit yourself to God. Trust me, being submissive is not always easy because many times, your flesh will want you to do otherwise. It is however part of your service to God.

The book of Esther presents to us the perfect example of a lady who understood the importance of being respectful. Mordecai ordered Esther not to tell the King, her husband that she was a Jew just yet. Please understand this. Esther was the queen, Mordecai was not even her real father, and she had the right to decide to go against his words and do whatever she felt like doing. But she obeyed and did according to what Mordecai told her to do because she respected and honoured his authority over her.

We can also deduce from the conversations that she had with the king that she was a queen who was submitted to her husband. Submission doesn't mean you are below or not up to the standard of the authority in question.

It will be a huge mistake for any lady to refuse to submit herself to God. You are nothing without God. He is the reason for your existence. He always has your best interest at heart when He tells you to do certain things. The Bible says before you were formed in the belly, God knew you and sanctified you (Jeremiah 1:5). So, to whose detriment would it be if you choose to disobey His commands?

Man's wisdom is useless and not all laws should be obeyed. Laws that do not glorify God are not to be obeyed! Exodus 1:17 tells us of the Hebrew midwives who disobeyed the law given by Pharaoh to kill all the sons of the Israelites because they feared God. As much as it is important for us to obey to all authorities, we must also be wise. Weigh all laws and orders using God's parameters! Do they agree with God's laws? Before you obey or submit yourself to doing anything, always ask yourself this question *"Would God be happy with me if I do this?"* If you search your heart and the scriptures, and the answer to that question is NO, then do not proceed in obeying such orders.

MY CONFESSIONS:

I, Queen (insert your name) confess that I am a woman under submission to God and every authority.

I understand that being submissive to my head doesn't make me any less of a woman.

I understand that submission as inconvenient as it may seem is part of my service to God.

Therefore, no matter where I find myself, obedience to God will always come first.

So, if any authority requires from me things that do not agree with God's word, I will not do it.

I choose to only do things that agree with the standard in God's word.

I am a queen under submission just as the church is under submission to Christ.

I will also pass on this quality to my offspring as it is my responsibility to train them up with the right mindset.

And I know that as long as I submit to God and to authority, everything will keep working in my favour and I will experience no downward slide.

AMEN

CHAPTER 3

QUEENS ARE COMPASSIONATE

"So Esther's maids and her chamberlains came and told her. Then was the queen exceedingly grieved; and she sent raiment to clothe Mordecai, and to take away his sackcloth from him: but he received it not" **(Esther 4:4)**

I am an advocate of Love. The world is full of so much hate. Progress cannot be made in a person or place where hatred dwells and that is why it is important that you are full of love and compassion wherever you find yourself. This is one quality we can draw from the life of Esther.

Having compassion simply means being understanding, having sympathy for someone who is in a fix or just in need of a shoulder to lean on. How do you feel when you walk on the street and you see someone begging for alms? At your working place, how do you react when one of your colleagues is in some kind of trouble? How compassionate are you?

Esther, when she was told by her maids about the plight of Mordecai, was moved with compassion and sent clothing to him to console him. You must have a compassionate spirit. In the very beginning, you were created as helpers! Genesis 2:18 says:

> *"And the Lord God said, it is not good that man should be alone; I will make him an help meet for him."*

You cannot help people if you don't have love in you and are not compassionate. You cannot even be a helper to your spouse if you are not compassionate with them. You must have and show compassion to as many that come in contact with you.

You show love when you are compassionate. You are not expected to be hostile to people around you. The Bible says in Hebrews 12:14 that you need to follow peace with all men. When Jesus was buried, it was women that went to His grave with spices to anoint His body because they were full of compassion (Mark 16:1-2). Also looking at the life of Dorcas in Acts 9: 36-43, she was so full of compassion that she used her skills to provide good works and charitable deeds to the people in Joppa. Her act of compassion was part of what gave her a second chance at life.

If Esther was not compassionate, her people, the Jews would have been wiped off the surface of the earth as was the wish of Haman. Her compassionate spirit saved her people from death.

In Proverbs 31:20, the Bible says the virtuous woman reaches out her hand to the poor and the needy! As a woman and a queen, you must learn to show love to people around you. If there is anything I've made up my mind to spend the rest of my life doing, it's to show love to anyone that comes in contact with me, after all, showing love is the whole essence of living as God is love!

MY CONFESSIONS:

I, Queen (insert your name) confess that I am full of love and compassion.

I am a child of God. God is LOVE; hence I am a child of LOVE!

I am a carrier of love and whoever comes in contact with me experiences the God kind of love.

No matter the circumstance I find myself in, I will let love speak first!

I refuse to be part of those that carry and spread hate.

Hate is not part of my embodiment.

I will not allow envy, pride and jealousy into my mind as they are the seeds that produce hatred in the heart of man.

I am committed to living the rest of my life full of compassion bearing in mind that I was created to provide help to those in need.

Just like Dorcas, I help those in need.

Even when I have little, I choose to provide help to those that have nothing.

I will also pass on this quality to my offspring as it is my responsibility to train them up with the right mindset.

I will also pass this down to as many that come in contact with me till the whole world radiates Love. AMEN

CHAPTER 4

QUEENS ARE WISE

"Then Esther bade them return Mordecai this answer, Go, gather together all the Jews that are present in Shushan, and fast ye for me, and neither eat nor drink three days, night or day: I also and my maidens will fast likewise; and so will I go in unto the king, which is not according to the law: and if I perish, I perish." **(Esther 4:15-16)**

Women are known to be wise and powerful. God has blessed us with so much wisdom, but the issue always seems to appear in the application of this wisdom. The ability of one to apply acquired knowledge is known as wisdom. As a queen, it is sacrosanct that you recognize this power and make the best use of it in every aspect of your lives. In the process, you shouldn't forget that true and complete wisdom comes from only God, not the number of degrees or exposure you may have acquired along the way.

After getting reports from her uncle, Mordecai about the schemes of Haman to wipe away her people, Queen Esther had to come up with a strategy to stop his plan. She quickly applied wisdom. The first step she took was too **fast and pray**. She knew such victory over a seemingly strong man like Haman would only come through prayer and fasting. So, she ordered that all the Jews join her to fast for three days and night. Then she made the bold move to approach the king, without invitation, damning the consequences. We cannot ignore the fact that it was her display of wisdom, by taking the matter to God, that granted her victory and favour before the King. When faced with challenges and adversities, it is safer to go to God directly for help and rely on wisdom from God, rather than our own human wisdom. What do we even know?

Let us consider Rahab as another beautiful example. She was another wise woman recorded in the Bible. Looking at her background, Rahab was not worthy of being mentioned in the Bible.

Rahab, despite being a prostitute, understood that God was a powerful God who dried up the Red Sea to deliver the Israelites from the Egyptians and so in the middle of what seemed to be an impossible situation, she made a seemingly foolish decision that earned her a place in the scriptures and eventually in the lineage of Jesus Christ. She was smart enough to realize that if she helped the Israelite spies, she and her family would be saved from death. So, she helped the spies to escape through her window with a rope. That foolish but wise impulsive decision saved her family from the death that accompanied the fall of the wall of Jericho.

Have you ever wondered why in the Book of Proverbs; wisdom is always likened to a woman? I believe it is because God has blessed women so much with wisdom. We just don't know it, and even if we do, many of us do not realize how much. Proverbs 31:26a says: *"she [a virtuous woman] opens her mouth with wisdom"* verse 27a also says *"She watches over the ways of her household"*. It takes wisdom to be able to watch over one's household successfully.

The mother of Belshazzar, the grandson of Nebuchadnezzar was another fast thinker and wise woman. Her son was faced with a very challenging situation and could not seem to find a solution to the problem. But she was able to think fast and proffer a solution – Daniel. Even looking at the life of Mary the mother of Jesus, we see another display of wisdom. When the wine finished at the wedding at Cana, Mary swiftly came to the rescue by informing Jesus and instructed that the disciples do whatever He says. At the end of the day, Jesus provided the best wine served at the wedding. (John 2:1-11).

MY CONFESSIONS:

I, Queen (insert your name) confess that I am an embodiment of wisdom!

I am a virtuous woman; I apply wisdom in all that I do.

I am a solution provider; I think fast and accurately in the midst of any challenge.

Because I am a woman filled with wisdom, I am priced far above rubies.

I do not speak as a fool nor dwell with fools.

I apply wisdom in making decisions that affect my family, career, personal lives.

I sit with King and Queens because I am one!

I open my mouth with wisdom and in my tongue is the law of kindness.

I understand that wisdom is the principal thing hence it becomes my emblem, I carry it wherever I go.

I act fast! I act with God's speed!

No matter what the situation is, I refuse to display any act of foolishness because I am full of Christ and he is the wisdom of God hence I am full of Wisdom.

AMEN

22

CHAPTER 5

QUEENS SPEAK THE RIGHT WORDS

"Then Esther the queen answered and said, If I have found favour in thy sight, O king, and if it please the king, let my life be given me at my petition, and my people at my request:

For we are sold, I and my people, to be destroyed, to be slain, and to perish. But if we had been sold for bondmen and bondwomen, I had held my tongue, although the enemy could not countervail the king's damage.

Then the king Ahasuerus answered and said unto Esther the queen, Who is he, and where is he, that durst presume in his heart to do so?"

The book of James tells us that if any man [woman] offend not in word, the same is a perfect man, and able also to bridle the whole body. This scripture and several others help us to understand the importance of using your mouth to speak the right words.

It is very important that you know how to use the right words when you come across anyone. You must be able to have conversations with people without getting into quarrels or arguments and even fights.

Whatever comes out of your mouth should be words that glorify God and create an atmosphere of peace.

Esther the queen, knew how to make use of the right words in relating her problems to the king. Let's look at it in a 21st century scenario.

Imagine a woman gets to find out that her husband's close friend is trying to influence her husband into divorcing her and getting another woman. How do you think she would confront her husband? Of course, you know all hell will let loose in that home. A typical woman will not go through the process of preparing a banquet for her husband and the close friend who is planning such evil. Neighbors will most likely rescue the husband from the clutches of his wife. No matter how pissed off you get about certain situations, you must be able to control yourself and not get offensive in the kind of words you use.

Sometimes, it's not just about the words you use, the tone with which you speak is also very important.

Esther was about to lose all her people, to a law that her husband approved. She could have decided to go into the king's chambers without being invited to nag, complain, and whine. Yet, she was able to control herself and think of a better way to approach the situation using graceful words.

As women, it is important that you speak and use words gracefully. Let the words that you speak bring and give life, let it heal, let it give joy rather than kill, cause pain or discord.

MY CONFESSIONS:

I, Queen (insert your name) will only use my mouth to say the right things.

No evil communication proceeds out of my mouth.

With my tongue, I give life not death.

I understand the importance of using the right words hence I am seasoned in my choice of words for communication.

When I speak, people get blessed, souls are won, and captives are freed.

My words are salt seasoned! No bitterness proceeds out of it.

Even when I am angry, I choose to keep silent than speak the wrong words.

With my words, I am able to win souls to Christ.

With my mouth, I prophesy and decree things that be not as though they were.

I understand words carry power hence; I weigh whatever I say,

If it is not edifying then it will not be said by me.

So, help me God. AMEN

CHAPTER 6

QUEENS NEVER NEGLECT THEIR OWN

"Then the king held out the golden sceptre toward Esther. So Esther arose, and stood before the king, And said, if it please the king, and if I have found favour in his sight, and the thing seem right before the king, and I be pleasing in his eyes, let it be written to reverse the letter devised by Haman the son of Haammedatha the Agagite, which he wrote to destroy the Jews which are in all the king's provinces" **(Esther 8:4&5)**

From the story of Esther, we learn a lot about having regard for our background and for people who have been in our lives since birth. Family is very important. This doesn't only cover our biological families, but also friends and loved ones.

Esther was an orphan who was taken up for adoption by her uncle Mordecai. We can also deduce from Bible's description, that Mordecai was not a very wealthy man. As a matter of fact, he was one of the captives of King Nebuchadnezzar. Having come from such a background, it could have been very easy for Esther to forget all about her background and all that she was before she became the queen. It would have been easy for her to get carried away with the wealth and pleasures the palace had to offer but this wasn't the case.

We see how Esther responded when she got reports from her uncle that Haman had made plans to wipe off her people, the Jews from the land. She ordered a three-day fast and with God's wisdom, she was able to win the heart of the king over to her side and stop Haman's evil plot to destroy her people.

There is a very big lesson to draw out from this. You must never forget where you come from even though your background or history is not and should not be a limitation to what you can accomplish in life.

A lot of women today want to "feel among" and so, they find themselves losing their essence just to fulfill the desires to meet up with the expectations of society. This has led many to living unfulfilled lives, and even taken some to their graves.

A lady must be proud of where she comes from. Your background doesn't have to put your back to the ground. No matter how bad you might feel it is, it is still the foundation of wherever and whatever you'd end up being in life. You just have to choose whether to let it affect you positively or negatively.

A lady must never deny her family because someday, she'd have her own family and wouldn't want to feel rejected by the ones she loves so dearly.

I know a lot of people have had terrible experiences in their families. Some have been deeply hurt by their parents, siblings, trusted friends, relatives, or acquaintances. This shouldn't make us deny what will forever be a part of us. As difficult as it may sound, you must learn to trust God enough to let go of things that have hurt you in the past, forgive those that have offended you and embrace the future. If the relationship was toxic and detrimental to your wellbeing, it's okay to keep your distance.

No matter what position you attain in life, you will always need family so you must learn to help them out when you are in a position to do so, you must learn to show love to your family.

When we look at the life of Esther, we see how the compassion she had for her people was able to deliver them from the evil Haman had mapped out for them.

Don't deny who you are because you are not proud of where you come from. Believe me, it doesn't put a limitation to where you are going to in life; a place of greater glory.

MY CONFESSIONS:

I, Queen (Insert your name) will never despise my background.

I will not look down on those that were there for me when the chips were down just because I have attained a higher status.

I also will not be too timid to launch out into the deep because I feel unqualified due to the background I come from.

I aim for greater things!

I will not allow my background to put my back to the ground.

I will always be of help to those in need as long as I am in a position to do so.

I refuse to let pride get the better part of me.

I will not ill-treat and maltreat those under me because I'm better placed than them.

I choose to let go of every hurt and pain memories that my past brings.

I choose to let go and look ahead to the bright future ahead.

I refuse to allow my past experiences to determine and limit my level of achievement.

I was made to do more! I was made to be more!

And all I was made to be, I shall become. AMEN

CHAPTER 7

QUEENS ARE HOSPITABLE

"And Esther answered, if it seem good unto the king, let the king and Haman come this day unto the banquet that I have prepared for him.
(Esther 5:5)

The word hospitality comes from the Greek word *"Philozenia"* which is a combination of two words- *Philos* which means affection and *zenos* which means stranger. So basically, hospitability simply means being affectionate towards strangers.

It is very easy to show affection to those you love and care about because you never want to see them hurt. What might seem difficult is being affectionate to your enemies or people you know nothing about. It takes the grace of God to do so.

Being hospitable towards others involves you opening your hands, hearts, and doors to any and every one in need.

Our reference scripture tells us how Esther invited the king and Haman to a buffet she prepared. It takes a really hospitable person to be able to cook and serve food to someone you know has an intention of wiping out their entire clan. Even though we understand that the buffet was all part of her plan to expose Haman and his wicked intentions to the king, you have to commend Esther for the level of hospitability she showed. She could have chosen to poison Haman's meal and silence him forever but she didn't. Instead, she invited him to a buffet twice and Haman had the feast of his life.

In Romans 12:13, Paul encourages believers to be given to hospitality. While some people do not find it tasking to be hospitable, some others do, especially introverts. However, God's grace is sufficient for all, so even if you find it difficult, don't stop trying to be hospitable, keep putting in efforts.

It's impossible for us not to have adversaries. Remember Psalm 23:5a says *"Thou preparest a table before me in the presence of my enemies...."*

I like to believe that the reason why God prepares a buffet for us in the presence of our enemies is so that we can share whatever it is he has laid on our tables with our enemies too, not just to "pepper them" as is the popular belief. A Christian practicing true hospitality plays a significant role in changing the world for good. How hospitable are you towards your enemies?

Hospitality involves kindness, 1 Peter 4:9 also admonishes us to show hospitality without grumbling. You're not being hospitable if you're doing what you do complaining and full of bitterness.

MY CONFESSIONS:

I, Queen (insert your name) am hospitable

To everyone I come in contact with.

I will not despise my neighbor and even my enemies.

I have an open heart, an open hand and open doors

I am hospitable even to those that hate me

I show hospitability without grumbling or complaining

Because I am full of kindness

I choose to be a true believer by practicing true hospitality come what may

Because I know with just my one act of hospitability, I can change my

Part of the world.

I yield myself to being used by God for all

His grace and love is more than sufficient for me

Therefore, I thrive as a queen full of the gift of hospitability.

AMEN

CHAPTER 8

QUEENS LIVE TO PLEASE THE KING OF KINGS

It is imperative that God finds pleasure in all you do. Sometimes, doing things that please God may not be convenient. It may require that you go out of your comfort zone but then again God's plan for you is not limited to a zone!

Sometimes, you will find yourself in a compromising situation and you might struggle on knowing how to go about it. It'll be a point where you have to choose to take a stand on good and evil. At such moments, let your zeal for the Lord and desire to make Him proud lead you to make the right decision. Ask yourself these questions- *Is this decision I am about to make in line with God's word? Will this action I am about to take please God?*

Personally, this question has helped me keep away from so many inappropriate things. I've lost friends, relationships and seemingly good offers because I asked myself the above question and I didn't get a reply in the affirmative. If it doesn't bring glory to God, count me out of it.

The truth is you cannot please everybody. Some people will not just like you no matter what you do to please them, so why bother? Place focus on pleasing the one that truly matters. Once He is pleased, every other thing falls into place.

MY CONFESSIONS:

I, Queen (insert your name) will live my life to please my King.

I will not lose focus on God just in a bid to do people-pleasing things.

If it is not going to please God, I am not willing to be a part of it.

If it is not going to bring glory to God, I will not be associated with it.

My life is and will always be a testimony of God's grace

I understand that one with the world is a failure but one with God means constant victory.

God finds and takes pleasure in all that I do.

I live a life of faith because I understand that without it,

It is impossible to please God.

I realize that in my bid to please God, I might need to do things that are not convenient for me but still, I will persevere because I am certain that at the end of the day, all things are working for my good

Because I love God and I am called according to His purpose.

AMEN

CHAPTER 9

WHAT IMPORTANT ATTRIBUTES DID QUEEN ESTHER DISPLAY?

Discipline

Discipline simply means a controlled behavior; a state of order.

If there is one thing my parents never tolerated from my siblings and I while growing up till this moment, it's indiscipline. My father would never hesitate to spank us 'in love' whenever we misbehaved.

> *"If ye endure chastening, God dealeth with you as with sons; for what son is he whom the father chasteneth not? But if ye be without chastisement, whereof all are partakers, then are ye bastards, and not sons.* **Hebrews 12:7&8**

This portion of the Bible talks about how important discipline is in the life of Christians. It says that any child left without discipline is illegitimate.

Esther was disciplined. How do we know this? The Bible tells us Esther required nothing extra but what was required when it was time to go see the king. It takes a lot of discipline to choose not to do extra especially when extra is available. It takes a lot of discipline to refrain from seemingly good things that are available to us but are not needed or necessary.

Another instance where Esther displayed discipline was in the area of fasting. Just in case you didn't know, in those days and even now, fasting is some form of spiritual discipline that requires one to abstain from food amongst other things for a period of time. People fast for different reasons. Some fast to gain direction on a particular situation, to seek wisdom, to prepare for ministry just as Jesus did, and to grow spiritually.

Esther fasted for three days and nights together with all the Jews. That is some high-level discipline if you ask me. Some of us cannot even stay away from food for just 3 hours talk more of half a day or a full day.

On this point of discipline, there are two levels; one where God disciplines us when we err or when it's needed to make us better, and then there's a place where we get to discipline ourselves to also make us better and to prevent us from erring. So, there is self-discipline and there is God's discipline. God commands self-discipline as seen in 1 Timothy 4:7. Either way, the importance of discipline cannot be over-emphasized in the life of a believer.

Proverbs 12:1 tells us that whoever loves discipline loves knowledge and that whoever hates reproof is stupid. Discipline is not always pleasant. Hebrews 12:11 says;

"For the moment of discipline seems painful rather than pleasant, but later it yields the peaceful fruit of righteousness to those who have been trained by it."

It is important that you yield yourself to discipline. An undisciplined person cannot go far in life. There is only so little you can achieve without discipline. It is the bridge between goals and accomplishments. It might not feel good at that time, but the end result is worth it!

Prayer

I'm sure you're all familiar with the song that says "Prayer is the key; prayer is the master key!"

I couldn't agree any less. If you claim to be a believer and you do not pray then you will live a life full of contradictions, this is something my pastor says a lot and it is true.

How does it feel being in a relationship with someone that never calls or texts you for days? Dejected, sad, and hurt, right? Now imagine how God feels when his bride refuses to communicate with Him!

Truth is, God does not benefit anything from your prayers. All the benefits of prayer come to you. Prayer simply means communicating with God and the Bible says that it should be done without ceasing. In the life of Esther, we see a woman sold out to prayer. The first thing she did in the face of trouble was a call for prayers because she understood the power she could access in the place of prayer. This should be your approach to every situation in life. How much have you prayed about that seemingly big situation you are faced with? Before you go ahead and start telling everyone that cares to listen, have you told God about it?

It is also important that you understand that prayer is a two-way thing. Imagine calling your partner and you are the only one that gets to talk, he doesn't say a word, nothing! That's how some of us communicate with God, we do all the talking. We don't give God any room to speak to us and HE WANTS TO SPEAK TO US.

When you pray, you should learn to give God time to speak. Most times, we're so caught up in all our needs and we think we have of what to say to God that we fail to listen to the solutions He gives us.

Your prayer life must be charged! Let's stop making excuses for being unable to pray. If you don't have time to pray then you're probably busier than God intended you to be. You are a queen! You are a warrior in heels (or sneakers, whichever you prefer)!

Courage

The life of Esther is one filled with an amazing level of courage. There is a difference between having strength and being courageous. Strength is the ability you need to make a move while courage is what you need to stay at it. Most of the time, what we have as humans is just strength not courage and that is why we see ourselves set out to achieve a particular goal and then mid-way, we fall out.

I can relate to this personally. I have a lot of projects I started because I felt I had the strength to pull it off but at the end of the day, I couldn't because I lacked the courage to.

Remember Joshua? When God called him to lead the people of Israel, God had to repeat to him several times to have strength and be of good courage. Courage is what keeps us going when the contrary wind comes. Courage expels fear. Courage in the Lord helps renew your strength when you become weak and weary. By strength shall no man prevail, strength is never enough (1 Samuel 2:9).

Esther was an orphan with nothing, she had no financial strength or power to achieve all that she achieved but she had the courage and her courage was found in God. Look at how she was able to stand face to face with her enemy (Haman) in the presence of the King and call him out for being an enemy of her people! That's great courage!

Some of us are so scared to face our fears because we lack the courage to. I pray in Jesus name, that as many as fall under this category receive their freedom even as they read this.

You have not been called to a life of fear! You have been called to a life of love, power and courage (sound mind).

Planning/Organization

Those that are close to me often caution me on how nonchalant and unorganized I can get most times about my personal space. Personally, I like to think it's one of the perks of being a creative. We tend to get easily distracted, we are unbothered about almost everything, our space always looks unorganized to others but in our head, it's actually organized because even in its scattered state, we know where all the stuff we need are placed. However, having read the story of Esther a few times, I am encouraged to begin to put conscious efforts into planning and organizing my life in general.

Esther was one queen who had a plan for every situation. She was the chief organizer of the plan that finally brought Haman to his downfall. For her, it didn't just stop at the idea generation stage, she saw it through to the execution stage because she had a plan mapped out. First, she had to come up with a spiritual plan of fasting and prayers for 3 days and nights, then she came up with the physical plan of meeting with the king to invite him to dinner.

I honestly believe Esther would not have been able to accomplish all of these, without having a plan to work with. She wouldn't have achieved all these with a high level of disorganization.

Most of the time, what hinders us from carrying out our plans and hinders us from fulfilling our purpose is nothing but procrastination and distractions. Many of us are in the habit of postponing things we can do immediately for a later period (which oftentimes, do not come). Somehow, these interruptions affect the number of goals we can reach.

It is important that you put in efforts into planning right and being highly organized. These will go a long way in helping you achieve your purpose and reach set goals.

MY FINAL NOTES

Having said all of these about Queen Esther, it is very important that I point the following out.

- Esther is not the standard, Jesus Christ is. As much as there is a lot to learn from the life of Esther as seen in preceding pages, you must understand that she is not the standard. Jesus Christ is the one and only perfect standard. He is your groom, the one to whom you are a queen.

- Esther being human definitely had her flaws. Even though these were not necessarily pointed out in the Bible. You however have a greater advantage; you have the Holy Spirit to guide you and teach you the right way to go. The Holy Spirit in you helps you to downplay your flaws, making you focus on your strengths and all that you have the power to achieve through Christ.

Your story doesn't necessarily have to end like Esther or Cinderella. In Esther's life, we see a battle between good and evil and good always wins! However, sometimes even when we do all the right things and have courage, the situation keeps getting worse making us wonder if God still exists and if He is still a good God. Yes, He is! Regardless of whatever it is we're going through; God remains a good God. Your situation will not change that fact.

Your situation might just be like that of John the Baptist who despite being the forerunner of Jesus and full of courage kept facing trials and tribulations till he was finally beheaded. Yet Jesus referred to him as the greatest of all men born by any woman (Matthew 11). God isn't looking at what the world sees, He looks at your heart. People will have probably looked at John the Baptist and mocked him saying the God he serves couldn't even save him from getting killed but God saw John's faithfulness!

Don't allow your situation make you lose faith. Your focus should be on your heavenly father and the treasures He has laid up for you where He is. Life on earth is fleeting and is as a smoke. Nothing really matters on this side. Just like the writer of the book of Ecclesiastes said, life is full of vanity; we came to this world with nothing and will return with nothing. What truly counts for the man in

Christ is not the riches of the world but his wealth in the cross.

Don't give up. The believer's life is not one that will be totally free from trials and tribulation; that's not what the Bible promises us. It however assures us that no matter what you are going through, God is always in it with you. He will not give you more than you can handle and ALL things are working together for your good because you love God and are called according to His purpose. So, your situation might not be good to you, but it is good for you! Just don't lose faith, you remain a queen regardless.

You might not be where you desire to be, but you are not where you used to be. Personally, I've tried to hold myself back from publishing this book because I do not have all the qualities I was led to write about in this book yet, but I am certain that He who began a good work in my life is able and faithful to complete it.

It is also very important to note that as Believing Queens, you function under the authority of your Lord and King, Jesus Christ. So, it is imperative that He is found to be at the center of all that you do. It is important that He is involved in every decision-making process you find yourself in.

Thankfully, He has given you His Holy Spirit to guide, teach, and correct you in all that you do. Of course, the functions of the Holy Spirit are not limited to the above.

You must never let your past experiences determine your future achievements. Just because you went through a terrible situation doesn't mean that your whole life has to revolve around that experience. Do not let your background set you back from being all that God has called you to be.

You are a queen specially made and designed for this generation and beyond. Don't let anyone or anything stop you from being who you are- **A QUEEN**.

QUEENING

www.ingramcontent.com/pod-product-compliance
Lightning Source LLC
Chambersburg PA
CBHW061300140726
47998CB00006B/2304